Unlimited JOY

Group Study and
Activation Guide

Kyllie Martin

Torn Curtain Publishing
Wellington, New Zealand
www.torncurtainpublishing.com

© Copyright 2023 Kyllie Martin. All rights reserved.

ISBN Softcover 978-0-473-67648-3
ISBN PDF 978-0-473-67649-0

When downloaded from the author's website, this study guide may be photocopied for personal and small-group use without specific permission from the publisher. However, this study guide may not be reproduced in full, stored in a retrieval system or transmitted in any form or by any means—electronic, mechanical, photocopy, recording or otherwise—or printed for commercial gain or distribution, without prior written permission from the publisher.

Quotations in this Study Guide are taken from 'Unlimited Joy' by Kyllie Martin.

Cover image by Vitaly Korovin. Used with permission.

A copy of this title is held at the National Library of New Zealand.

Welcome!

Thank you for joining me for this *Unlimited Joy* group study. I am so glad that you made the decision as a community to delve into this topic and activate joy in your own life. The joy of the Lord is a gift to strengthen us and others! I pray you will encounter the Holy Spirit in a new and deeply personal way, and that He will pour His oil of gladness upon you in ever-increasing measure!

Bless you,
Kyllie

Getting Started

The purpose of this study is to help you:

- Learn about the promise of joy in the Bible
- Raise your expectation for joy in your life
- Understand how to process grief with the Holy Spirit and exchange mourning for joy
- Discover different ways to activate joy in your life and share it with others

How to use this study:

This study guide is designed to be used in conjunction with the book, *Unlimited Joy: Accessing all that is Promised* by Kyllie Martin.

There are fourteen chapters in the book. Participants are asked to read one chapter each week and complete the activation section at the end of the chapter. The only exception to this is week 12, when we combine two chapters.

The group session is a time to dive deeper using the discussion questions in this guide and to share what God is doing in your life in the area of joy. As a group, decide whether you will meet weekly, fortnightly, or monthly (about 1 ½ hours for each session is a good idea). If the group is pressed for time, leaders may choose to select the most appropriate questions for each session. Likewise, since each chapter is designed to stand alone, the group may decide to study a selection of chapters rather than the whole book.

To end your group discussion, close in prayer using the prayer prompt at the end of each week's questions.

Preparing for your first meeting:

- Arrange a venue and suggested meeting time
- Invite participants (8-10 per group is suggested)
- Order a book for each participant (or each person may wish to purchase their own). Be sure to allow time for delivery. Books are available in both paperback and eBook versions via Amazon.com or at www.kylliemartin.com/unlimited-joy
- Decide the format of each session—will one person lead, or will participants take turns facilitating? Will you have refreshments (tea, coffee, supper etc.)?
- If your group have not previously met each other, you may choose to hold an initial 'meet and greet' before the first session.

Week 1

Chapter One: Joy Unexpected

Discussion Questions

1. How are you feeling about this study? Are you excited about it, or are you feeling reluctant?

2. Discuss your thoughts and feelings about the unusual 'incident' which happened to Kyllie in the auditorium on pages 2-3. Share your feelings and/or reluctance towards Holy Spirit joy and laughter.

3. What are your experiences of the joy of the Lord? Have you encountered joy like this before, and if you have, what has your experience been?

4. Do you feel hungry for more joy in your life? Why, or why not? In which area(s) of your life would you like to experience joy (or more joy)? How might your life look different if you experienced more joy?

5. Is there someone you know or have met who seems to carry greater levels of joy than most? In what way does their joy make you to want what they have?

6. After reading the first chapter and completing the activation, have you experienced any increase in joy? Share your testimonies.

Prayer

Start asking the Lord for more joy. As a group, you may like to pray the prayer Kyllie prayed (p 6):

> *"How tediously persistent you have been in my life! Oh Lord, if only I could have had tediously persistent joy through struggles. Lord, crown me with everlasting joy! I want to be overtaken with gladness so that sorrow and sighing will flee."*

If anyone has shared testimonies of increased joy, invite them to lay hands on others in the group and ask God to release joy into their lives as well.

Week 2

Chapter Two: The Promise of Joy

Discussion Questions

1. How have you seen joy being taught in the church? Would you say it is spoken of often and encouraged, or only taught in relation to trials? In your experience, is joy generally thought of as a choice, or as something the Holy Spirit can activate?

2. How have you traditionally defined joy? What was your reaction to the definitions that Kyllie read (p. 18)?

3. What were your thoughts towards the following questions Kyllie asked regarding the work of the enemy (p 19)?:

   Had he lied to us about joy? Had he destroyed our understanding of joy, making us content with peace and hope, or trying to find it in our own strength? Had he stolen our expectation of how much joy is truly available in the Christian life? I wondered if he had waged war on our joy because he knows that the joy of the Lord is our strength. Was there a strength to be found that he didn't want us to access? . . . Was the enemy purposely trying to steal our joy because he knows how effective and compelling it is, and what a powerful evangelistic tool it is?

4. Look up the following references about the promise of joy and read them aloud. You may like to declare them together!

   John 15:11, Isaiah 35:10, Isaiah 51:11, Isaiah 61:1-4, 7, Romans 14:17, and Luke 17:21

5. Read Revelation 21:3-4 and discuss the question: "Why would we need joy in heaven?"

6. After reading chapter two and completing the activation, did the Holy Spirit identify any lies you have been believing regarding joy? What is your expectation for joy now?

Prayer

As a group, spend some time praying for the Lord to increase your hunger and expectation for joy. Ask Him to pour it out on the group over the coming week. If group members have already experienced greater joy, ask them to pray for others in the group, that the Lord will increase everyone's joy levels together!

Week 3

Chapter Three: The Person of Joy

Discussion Questions

1. Kyllie mentioned that during hardship she clung to the Lord, but it presented a surprising challenge: when the hardship reduced, so did her closeness to Him. What has been your experience regarding your relationship with the Lord during good times vs hard times? When do you find it easiest to be close to Him?

2. When you are learning things about God, do you focus more on God's principles or presence? Can you share anything that has helped you connect with the Lord better?

3. How do you think God feels about us going to Him only for what we can get rather than to simply spend time with Him?

4. As you read chapter 3, did you notice anything from the story of the prodigal son that you hadn't seen or heard before?

5. Discuss your experience with the activations at the end of this chapter. Which one of the Trinity did you behold? What was your experience?

Prayer

As a group, take some time to quietly reflect on the Hebrew word for presence, *paniym* (meaning 'face'), from the root word *pana* (meaning, to turn). You may like to set the atmosphere by playing a worship song such as *I Love Your Presence* by Bethel Music. Behold the Lord together, 'turning towards His face' and asking God's presence to come.

Week 4

Chapter Four: The Position of Joy

Discussion Questions

1. Describe your church background in relation to the Holy Spirit. Was the Holy Spirit emphasized in your denomination? Have you primarily encountered Him as a 'still quiet voice', or one who comes in presence and power?

2. Kyllie shared the teaching she received in a class called, *The Amazing Power of In.* (p 36). How does this teaching change your view of Jesus' illustration in John 15 of the vine and the branches? Things you could discuss include: plugging in, grafting, what parts are the vine (two-sided vs one-sided connection), abiding isn't hard, harsh pruning vs gentle cleansing, authoritarian gardener vs nurturing gardener.

3. How do the Hebrew and Greek meanings of the word *abide* help shape your expectations of a relationship with God?

    English: to remain, live or dwell
    Hebrew: interpersonal relationships, cohabitation
    Greek: continuing to stay

4. Share any lies (or revelations) that the Holy Spirit revealed to you during the process of reading this chapter and completing the activations.

5. Discuss the different ways that you have experienced the presence of the Lord and actively abided in Him this week.

Prayer

As a group I invite you to spend some connecting with the Lord. You may like to set the atmosphere by playing a worship song such as *Rest On Us* by Maverick City. Ask the Holy Spirit to reveal himself in new ways.

Week 5

Chapter Five: Overflowing Joy

Discussion Questions

1. Together read from page 46 from "One day I asked the Lord a question . . ." until halfway down page 47. Discuss the prophetic picture of "the oil of gladness being poured out until the vessels are filled".

2. Look up and read aloud the following scriptures on 'all joy', the 'fullness of joy' and 'abounding joy'.

    Psalm 16:11, John 15:11, Acts 13:52 NASB, 2 Corinthians 7:4 and Romans 15:13

3. Why do you think there is this emphasis on abundant joy in Scripture?

4. On page 47, Kyllie wrote about the different words used for joy and rejoicing and how there are many different expressions of joy during different seasons. Discuss your current expression of joy or rejoicing. Are there other expressions you would like to have or display during the season you are in?

5. Can you think of any ways the enemy has tried to disqualify you with respect to joy?

Prayer

Ask the individuals to identify anyone in the group who carries an expression of joy they would like to see in their own lives. Then invite them to lay hands on the others and pray that the Holy spirit would impart what they carry upon them also.

Week 6

Chapter Six: Joy and Trust

Discussion Questions

1. In this chapter Kyllie writes about knowing God and being known by God. How well do you feel you know God? To what extent do you feel known by God?

2. Kyllie draws on the Hebrew word *yada* to show that trust isn't about trying harder but about coming to a place of greater intimacy with the Lord. How did this insight about the word *yada* bring greater revelation to Proverbs 3:5-6?

This week, discuss your thoughts around *yada* and trust. You may like to separate into smaller groups to allow more time to share. Take turns to share openly with the group about the things that you are struggling to trust the Lord with. Share your fears and worries about trusting God in your group and what key you have identified to activate this season. Allow others to encourage you with testimony from similar situations or to speak prophetically or pray for your situation.

Week 7

Chapter Seven: Joy for Mourning

Discussion Questions (You may like to divide into smaller groups to allow more time to share)

1. What thoughts and feelings did this chapter bring up for you?

2. Did you connect with something particular that Kyllie wrote about in this chapter?

3. Were there any lies you identified that you have been believing in relation to grief?

4. To what extent do the promises you know from the Bible about mourning and joy line up with your beliefs?

5. Discuss your thoughts on the paragraph from page 67, being sensitive to people in the group, "I have pondered my workmate's statement afresh. Is it true that some losses are impossible to get over, or is that merely a lie we have been led to believe that no one wants to challenge? Do we not believe it because we haven't seen it?"

6. How have you grieved in the past, and did anything from the Jewish mourning traditions outlined in this chapter challenge your mourning practices?

7. Do you feel like you are a prisoner or captive to grief? If so, have you identified that you may have a spirit of heaviness?

8. How did you go with the activation this week? Does anyone have a testimony to share?

Pray for and minister to each other with the help of the Holy Spirit in relation to anything these questions brought up.

Alternative Option: Lead the group in a time of activation. Play the song *Lean Back* by Capital City Music and invite participants to imagine themselves leaning back into the arms of Jesus and him washing ashes from their hair with the oil of gladness.

Week 8

Chapter Eight: Sowing in Tears

Discussion Questions

1. The topic of this chapter can be quite a sensitive subject, and this teaching is not commonplace. What did you wrestle with as you read this chapter? Divide into smaller groups if necessary to allow more time to share.

2. Share about an area of your life that you are lacking hope in (and that you wrote your prophetic song about). Read your song to the group, then discuss how you found the process of writing the song and how you felt afterwards. Did it bring hope to your situation?

3. Identify an area of your life where you need greater hope. Get each participant to share that area. If there are similarities in the group, get people to pair up or get into small groups. (i.e finances, prodigal children, illness, reconciliation in relationships etc). Spend some time finding scriptures that declare truth and hope into that situation and write some declarations to speak over your life this week.

Prayer

Spend time praying for each other's situations.

As a larger group, play the song *Fear Is Not My Future* by Brandon Lake with the volume turned up! Sing out loud together, saying goodbye to fear and welcoming peace and joy.

Week 9

Chapter Nine: A Pathway Back to Joy

Discussion Questions

1. How did you find the process of writing a prayer of lament? Is this something you have done before? Were there any sections of the process you found hard?

2. Discuss in small groups your response to some of the questions in the activation:

    Turn Quickly - *Are there any substances or unhelpful habits you find yourself turning to, to help you avoid the pain of grief? Do you run to God quickly, or run to Him after trying everything else?*

    Complain Freely - *Are you someone who tends to stay stuck in complaint? Are you still complaining about things that happened in the past which haven't been processed or forgiven? Or do you feel you can't complain to God?*

    Ask Boldly - *Do you struggle to ask the Lord for what you need? Why or why not? Do you see God as a good Father who provides for His children? Is there a lie you are believing about His character or His love for you?*

Trust Fully - *How easily can you trust the Lord with the situation you have lamented? If you are struggling with this, why do you think this is?*

Prayer

Spend time praying for each other.

Week 10

Chapter Ten and Eleven: The Banquet Table & Shouting for Joy

(This week's activities may be outside some participants' comfort zone but I would encourage you to seek the Lord on what parts to incorporate)

Get together for a 'Joy Party'

Start with the song *Come and Let Your Presence* by Austin Johnson to set the atmosphere for the night.

Explain to the group that you (the leaders) are going to do a prophetic act to start the evening, and as in Psalm 23, anoint the guest's heads with oil to wash away the dust from the long weary road.

Go around the group and share briefly (perhaps in one sentence depending on the size of the group) what area of your life where you need breakthrough or healing. Spend some time prophesying into each other's lives.

Pick some joyful songs, turn up the stereo or speaker loudly, and spend some time together dancing, shouting for joy, and praising the Lord, believing that He is fighting for you. While you are dancing and singing, 'drink up in the spirit'!

Here are some song suggestions:

- *God Turn It Around* by Jon Reddick (Bethel Music)
- *Come Alive* by Hillsong
- *This Is What You Do* by Bethel Music
- *Joy Endlessly* by Souvenirs Worship
- *Tangible Joy* by Jonathan Helser

Week 11

Chapter Twelve: Joy Thieves

Discussion Questions

This chapter talks about some of the physical, psychological and spiritual aspects that can steal your joy. Share with the group the things that you identified that often steal your joy and discuss the action steps that you are putting into place. If you identified more than one thing, discuss where you are going to start. If anyone in the group needs healing in any area of their life, pray for them.

Alternate option: Be Childlike Challenge

One thing that can steal our joy is responsibility (and not having enough time for play). Kids laugh up to 400 times a day compared to an adult's average of 40 times a day. This week, identify a fun activity that you could do together. Some options include: going to a trampoline park, playing on a playground together, racing go-carts, playing some kids' games, or having a children's party—anything that's not too serious! The idea is to be childlike, and hopefully laugh lots.

Week 12

Chapter Thirteen: Joy, Our Strength

Discussion Questions

Since the context of this week's chapter is connected with Nehemiah 8:10 and feasting ("eating the fat and drinking the sweet") a suggestion is to meet for a meal and share your testimonies over food. This week, take time to celebrate, release gratitude and share testimonies. Start by reflecting on the questions that you answered in weeks one and two:

1. Are there any areas of your life where you need more joy and happiness?

2. How might your life look different if you experienced more joy?

3. What is your current expectation for joy?

Now reflect on what has changed since the start of this study.

4. How has joy increased in your life?

5. What encounters have you had with the Holy Spirit that have released joy in your life or caused you to exchange mourning for joy?

6. Have you shared what you have been reading with other people? What changes have you seen in their lives?

Prayer

Pray for each other, laying hands on one another and releasing the joy you carry into each other's lives.

Week 13

Chapter Fourteen: The Restoring Power of Joy

Discussion Questions

1. For the final activation, you were asked to journal about being an oak of righteousness who stands with strength and longevity, and to visualize the lives who were being rebuilt as a result of the double portion you have received. Share some of the things you wrote about.

2. What most stood out to you while reading this book and completing this study? Are there any activations that you will continue doing to foster joy in your life?

3. Identify two or three people who you think need more joy in their lives. Discuss ways you could share joy with them. Pray together as a group for those people you have identified.

Before finishing this session, have someone read this declaration over the group:

> *I raise my flask over your head and pour out the oil of joy. Here, in the Father's presence, I declare that fullness of joy abounds. As He releases rejoicing over you, I raise my voice in agreement. I declare that Zion is your native home! Songs of joy surround you, and gladness*

overtakes you. Gone are the days of sowing in tears—the time has come for you to reap with joy. I release a shout of triumph over you. Grief is conquered; the enemy is destroyed. Your chains have fallen off! Walk out of captivity and into the joy of the Lord. A double portion is your inheritance! You have joy enough to sustain your family, your church, your nation! I bless you with all joy. You have become a display of His splendor!

Alternate option: Go into your neighborhood or community and do some street ministry together, sharing the joy that you have received. Freely you have received; now freely give! Here are a few options that work well in a public place:

- Hold signs saying 'free hugs +/- prayers'. Release joy as you hug people and pray for them.
- Draw a large circle with JOY written inside it. Spend some time worshiping and praying into that space, and then invite people in to receive joy.
- Identify people who you would love to share this message with and invite them to an *Unlimited Joy* study. Arrange books, a time, date, and venue. Be part of an outbreak of joy!

From Kyllie

Thank you so much for investing in the *Unlimited Joy* book and study. I hope you have been blessed as you have read, discussed, and activated joy over the past 13 weeks. I would love to hear testimonies of how you have encountered the joy of the Lord in your life and what a difference it has made to you and to those around you.

Send me a message or share your testimony on my social media or website:

@kylliemartinauthor
hello@kylliemartin.com
www.kylliemartin.com

www.ingramcontent.com/pod-product-compliance
Lightning Source LLC
Chambersburg PA
CBHW062044290426
44109CB00026B/2725